ABRAHAM'S SEED

Promise, Covenant, Inheritance

Cheptoo Morei.

Independently Published
Nairobi, Kenya

To You.

Table of Contents

Table of Contents v

Preface vii

Part 1: Abraham's Walk with God.

Introduction : Who was the man Abram?.....................3

The Separation Preparation. 7

Altars 12

I Will Curse Him That Curseth Thee… 14

Very Rich in Cattle, in Silver, and in Gold. 17

Not Everybody can Come. 20

…Unto A Land That I Will Shew Thee. 23

Warfare..26

Fear Not...31

Lord, I have A Question… 33

Giving God a Hand...37

Be Thou Perfect- The Covenant, the Circumcision...40

Entertaining Angels- Is Anything Too Hard for The Lord? 45

The Righteous Shall Never Be Forsaken....................49

The Fear of God is not in this Place…I thought........53

At The Set Time. 56

Because He Is Thy Seed..57

A Covenant with God As The Witness. 59

A test- Jehovah-Jireh. 62

A Death, a Burying Place. 66

Blessed In All Things. 69

A Command Given, and A Prayer Answered..........71

The Lord Led Me. 75

The Pitch- The Testimony. 78

A Bride for Isaac. 80

Abraham Is Gathered Up..................83

Part 2: The Fulfilment of God's Promises to Abraham.

The Appropriation Principle..................87

God's Promises to Abraham..................90

How The Promises Were Fulfilled to Abraham. 94

Part 3: We Are Abraham's Seed and Heirs of The Promise.

How We Came To Be..................103

Christ Our Qualifier..................107

Jesus Christ the Son of Abraham..................110

We are Abraham's Seed. 112

How We Obtain The Promise..................117

The Manifestation of the Promise in Our Lives. 121

Conclusion..................127

Bibliography..................130

<u>Preface</u>

As I reflect on the evolution of this book, from its inception in February 2023 to its current state in February 2024, I am struck by the profound shift in its essence. What began as a journey toward Christian maturity has blossomed into something far deeper — a quest for true rest in the arms of our Heavenly Father.

Imagine stepping into a realm where striving ceases, and peace reigns supreme. That's the essence of the journey I **invite** you to embark upon. It's about embracing the example of Christ Himself, who walked in perfect harmony with His Father's will, always about His Father's business.

This journey isn't about confusion or aimlessness; it's about finding clarity and purpose in every step. It's about trading fear for courage, lack for abundance, and weakness for strength. It's about entering into a place of divine provision and grace that knows no bounds.

I hope that as you journey through these pages, you'll experience a profound sense of rest in your mind and heart. May you be inspired to pursue Kingdom business with dedication, excellence, and love in every endeavor.

This book is an invitation to engage with truth on a personal level. Through interactive devotional exercises, I invite you to journey alongside me, not merely seeing through my eyes, but seeking out Jesus — the living word — that speaks directly to your soul.

As you pray, *"Give us this day our daily bread,"* may these pages become a feast for your spirit, nourishing you with the bread of deliverance and restoration; because we already have within us what we seek. And as you journey to the final page, may your heart overflow with the assurance of a powerful testimony, a testament to the transformative power of rest in the arms of our loving Father.

Without wax,
Cheptoo Morei.

Part 1:

Abraham's Walk

with God.

Introduction : Who was the man Abram?

Genesis 11:25- 32

Genesis chapters 10 and 11 are a story and genealogy of the generations which came from the sons of Noah, after the flood. It also tells us of the story of the tower of Babel and how the Lord intervened in order to continue his purpose for humanity on the earth of spreading and establishing dominion throughout the earth. The story of Abram begins in Genesis 11:25 by mentioning his father Terah who had him at the age of seventy and two sons, Nahor and Haran after him. They lived in their native land of Ur of the Chaldees, and it is where the middle brother Nahor died. Abram was a native of Ur of the Chaldees and at that time in history Ur was one of the commerce and culture hubs in the Middle East. Abram's name means high father or exalted father, and in its appearance in archaeological discoveries it is associated with priesthood and spiritual authority.

It is estimated that Ur was an area in lower Mesopotamia and in the time of Terah was under the new Sumero-Akkadian Empire of Ur Nammu, the founder of the famous third empire of Ur. Terah led his family out of Ur when it was entering its heyday of commercial and political prestige (Unger). In Genesis 11:31 Terah took his son Abram, his wife Sarai, and his grandson Lot and left Ur of the Chaldees where they dwelt intending to go into the land of Canaan. They however got to a place called Haran and they dwelled there where Terah the patriarch of the family died and was buried. The story is elaborated more in Acts 7:2- 4, it makes it clear that the God of glory had appeared to Abram while in Ur and instructed him to leave and go to a place that He will show him and there He would bless him.

"And he said, Men, brethren, and fathers, hearken; the God of glory appeared unto our father Abraham, when he was in Mesopotamia, before he dwelt in Charan, And said unto him, Get thee out of thy country, and from thy kindred, and come into the land which I shall shew thee. Then came he out of the land of the Chaldeans, and dwelt in Charan: and from thence, when his father was dead, he removed him into this land, wherein ye now dwell."
-Acts 7:2-4

The instruction was as it is recorded in Genesis 12:1-3 but initially Terah was only comfortable with moving the family as far out as Haran. Haran was a flourishing city as well, located in a trade route, and was also the centre of worship of the moon god Sin=- (Unger). Whether Terah was drawn to Haran for a commercial or a spiritual reason is a debate, what we know is that God gave the instruction to Abram, who relayed it to the rest of the family. It is in Haran, the city with the same name as his dead son, the city that offered him comfort and a place of remembrance that Terah died. After his death, Abram became the new head of the family; he remembered the original instructions from God and set off to honour it. They set off and went into the land of Canaan, when they got there the Lord began to speak to Abram of the plan, the future, and His intended purpose stretching forth into eternity.

The scriptures continue to tell us that Abram walked with the Lord all the days of his life and when he went to his grave, he left to his son the greatest inheritance; the Lord, the Fear of Isaac. From Isaac's son, Jacob the Lord's nation was chosen and established. Out of the tribe of Judah, Christ/the Messiah was born and by His sacrifice on the cross, man was made to reign with God once again. Those who are saved by grace through faith are restored to their original position of having dominion on earth, over the fish of the sea, and over the fowl of the air, and the cattle, and all the earth, and over every creeping thing that creepeth upon the earth. (Genesis 1:26) The appropriation of this is through the patriarch Abraham, who obtained the promise from God by faith, and by faith all Christians are his seed and therefore heirs of the promises and keepers of the covenant. But the question is always *"How do I obtain the promise? How does it become the reality in this life I'm living? How do I reconcile my present to God's promises over my life?"* The answer is in the word of God, and we'll discover it here. Those with eyes will see, and ears will hear.

<u>The Separation Preparation.</u>

Genesis 12:1-5

God was looking for a man in that generation with whom he could partner to influence earth and creation. He had found Abram to be a man with the right heart posture, the right attitude, and the right faith; so He had begun relating with him. After he mourned his father, Abram remembered God and decided to follow through on their agreement. The first condition for the beginning of their relationship was him obeying the word of the Lord and taking a physical step as a demonstration of his surrender and obedience to this spiritual being that he had met only as the God of glory.

*"Now the Lord **had said** unto Abram, Get thee out of thy country, and from thy kindred, and from thy father's house, unto a land that I will shew thee: And I will make thee a great nation, and I will bless thee, and make thy name great; and thou shalt be a blessing: And I will bless them that bless thee, and curse him that curseth thee: and in thee shall all families of the earth be blessed. So Abram departed, as the Lord had spoken unto him; and Lot went with him: and Abram was seventy and five years old when he departed out of Haran. And Abram took Sarai his wife, and Lot his brother's son, and all their substance that they had gathered, and the souls that they had gotten in Haran;*

and they went forth to go into the land of Canaan; and into the land of Canaan they came."
-Genesis 12:1-5

God is Almighty, Supreme, and cannot change; we as human beings are to change and adjust to relate with Him. God did not tell him where he would end up; only that he had to leave to live. The Lord's word is final, authoritative, and supreme, with the power necessary to create that which is spoken. The same '*said*' that created the earth and formed the foundations of the universe is the same '*said*' that IS every time He speaks. Our faith and the actions we take based on the faith and fear of the Lord in us is what proves (makes certain and successful) the word of the Lord in our lives. That is why the Lord Jesus said, If you pray believing, you have received (Mark 11:24).

The Lord in this authority spoke and commanded Abraham to leave his country (physical location), his kindred (family and community), and his father's house (place of authority and submission) and go to a land that He would show him. That condition for the relationship was connected to a promise:

- I will make of you a great nation,
- And I will bless you;
- I will make your name great,
- And you shall be a blessing.
- I will bless those who bless you,
- And curse the one who curses you;

- And all the families of the earth shall bless themselves by you.

To leave his country- In the 16th and 17th Century, when the first Bible translations to English were done, a Country was a geographical area under the rule of a monarch, with lords who were subject to them. The lords owned property and the poorer in the society worked for the lords and the monarchical family. Countries also had boundaries that shifted depending on the degree of power to expand that certain country had. They had a set of rules common to all, paid tribute to the lord or prince in charge, and traded and interacted with neighbouring countries. When the Lord told Abraham to leave his country, it was the geographical location that he lived in under the ruler ship of a certain lord or king, where all adhered to a set of rules agreed upon by the lords/elders of the land and paid tribute to the king. He was leaving the gods and kings of the land, the customs and traditions of the land, and the economic, social, and political systems of the country.

To leave his kindred- He was instructed to leave his family and relations. They could be related by blood or under common beliefs and customs and live in a close geographical area, like a town or village. They represent an area of common systems, practices, and an order of administration and authority. God had instructed him to leave and be his own man so that they could relate independent of other people's influence.

To leave his father's house- A father's house is the closest place of interaction and submission for a son.

When someone is in his father's house he is still under the rule and authority of his father. He worships as his father worships; he does as instructed, and lacks autonomy in decision making. Independence is not achieved when the father dies, but when the son makes the conscious decision and effort to disconnect himself from the altars, customs, practices, and beliefs that are inherited generationally. This is why Abram found it difficult to follow it through the first time, and after his father died, he still asked if any of his father's house would go with him, and Lot agreed. God wanted Abram in a place where He, Jehovah, would be his all and in all, a place of total surrender to the authority, ruler ship, and counsel of The Lord.

He took Sarai, all their substance, all their servants and slaves, and they departed for Canaan, and his nephew Lot went with him. The Apostle Paul writes and says that Abram followed God's word not knowing where he was going (Hebrews 11:8); he went only with the word that God would show him the land where he was going. As we go on, we will begin to see the growth of this relationship between God and Abram, how the promises manifested in his life, beyond his lifetime, and how we all fit into this beautiful canvas, by God's design. God takes you through experiences to strengthen your faith and for you to learn more about Him: to know Him more and to love Him more, because love grows with knowledge.

We shall through our study seek to explore and present how each of these promises were fulfilled, in and out of time, during Abraham's lifetime and beyond it, and how it all fit into the greater plan of God for mankind.

❖ Do you think Abraham obeyed God's instructions fully?

....

....

....

❖ What attributes of God do we learn from the story so far?

....

....

....

....

❖ Have you ever been in a situation where you believed God had instructed you to move? .... Did you obey it?

....

Altars

Genesis 12:6-9

Abram and his companions went into the land of the Canaanites, into the place of Sichem, the plain of Moreh. In this area, the Canaanites occupied the land. The Lord again appeared to him in this land and said: *"Unto thy seed will I give this land."(12:7)*

And as Abram believed God's word, there he built **an altar of covenant,** unto the Lord who appeared to him. It is important to always mark out places of remembrance to the dimension of God you have met in a season, an unforgettable monument to the character of God that has been revealed to you in the interaction you have had. It is also a mark of humility when people does not yet have a full sum of what was promised but is grateful for the little they have received; it opens up the way for more to flow towards them. Abram had left his country behind, his land, on God's promise to take him to another land, and on that day God assigned it to him. HE built an altar to remind him and all future generations that their God keeps His word.

People occupied the area where he had originally planned to pitch his so he kept travelling through the land, and because he needed further direction from the Lord he built an altar. In a land between Bethel and Hai, Abram built **an altar of faith** and called the Lord by His name. The second altar was a declaration by Abram that *"finally, I have seen whom I have* *believed."* He had finally gotten to the point where the reality of God was always present with him, and he depended on God to order his steps. From there he journeyed further south towards Negeb in stages.

Questions.

❖ Have you seen whom you have believed? Describe
Him...
....
....
....
....

❖ Who did Abram know God as?

....
....
....
....

I Will Curse Him That Curseth Thee...

When God said ***"and I will…"***, everything that came after was done as far as he was concerned; only the manifestation in the physical was bidden, but isn't that what faith is?

Canaanites were occupying all the fertile grazing lands of the plains of Canaan so Abram and his household travelled further south towards the less populated mountainous regions. In these regions grazing fields were not as bounteous so soon he had to move. He decided within himself to move his household down to Egypt to live out the famine; there is no indication in the scriptures that God of faith were involved in him making that decision; just experience and need.

As they were entering Egypt, he concocted a plan to keep his head, and maybe in the process make him richer. He knew that his wife Sarai was beautiful, and he knew that men like and will kill for beautiful women, so he convinced his wife to tell everyone that she was his sister so the Egyptians would not attempt to kill him to get her. In those days women and children would be taken as spoils of war. If on the other hand people thought they were siblings, then any man who was interested in taking her as a wife would have ended up giving cattle, gold and silver to Abram as dowry for her hand. That is what happened; when the Pharaoh's courtiers saw how beautiful she was, they told Pharaoh of her and she was *"taken into Pharaoh's house"*. Just like that, she joined the Pharaoh's harem: a mark of wealth in society, even today is having the most beautiful women as yours. To show appreciation and seal the union, Pharaoh gave Abram sheep, oxen, he asses, menservants and maidservants, she-asses and camels. Abram became even richer than he was when he left Haran.

God had to intervene: remember when a man and a woman get married, the word of the Lord says that the two become one, therefore any covenant God had with Abram was also attached to Sarai. Pharaoh could not have her, because that would interfere with God's purpose and plan before it even began taking root. The Lord was angry and plagued Pharaoh's house for Abram's sake: not because Abram was a good man but because he was God's representative here on earth. The one thing he had done right was enter into covenant with Yahweh. Did He not say He would curse those who curse him?

The Egyptians were an extremely superstitious people in those days, so I would conclude that the Pharaoh called his magicians, astrologers, witches, and wise men, and together they discovered that the plagues were because he had taken Abram's wife and Abram's God was mightier than all their gods. So the Pharaoh sent Abram away with all that he had, and even sent his men to ensure that Abram truly left his lands. He left

Egypt richer and stronger than he went in; in possessions, power, and faith.

This story is also a foreshadowing of what ended up happening with the children of Israel when they were led out of Egypt by Moses- even then, the Pharaoh told them to Go!- It is also a parallel to what happened in the end of Matthew 8, when the people of Gergesenes begged Jesus to leave their land because His going there had upset their altars and their gods.

Questions.

❖   Have you had any experiences in your life that have served to strengthen your faith?

....

....

....

❖ Do you think what Abram did in the situation was right?
Justify...

....

....

....

....

Very Rich in Cattle, in Silver, and in Gold.

Genesis 13:1-4

After they left Egypt, Abram, and his companions went into the south to Negeb and from there he travelled in stages back into Bethel, where he had first pitched his tent. While Abram was on his travels, the Lord was expanding and increasing him, to the point where he *"was <u>very rich</u> in cattle, in silver and in gold."* Yet he felt that something was lacking; after he called the Lord by name, he went down and started walking by his own strength and imagination, after he had been unceremoniously chased out of Egypt, he worked his way back to the last point where everything seemed to be right.

Abram was a travelling nomad. Nomads do not have permanent homes, they traverse the land with their families, cattle, and all their substance; looking for grazing pastures and water, trading with other people for various wares along the way, and interacting with all they come into contact with socially such as in marrying, community activities and even worshipping. They camp in spots where water and pastures are readily available, where there aren't previous occupants on the spot and if there are they do not mind sharing, the place is easily fortified and defended against potential attacks and there are trade routes nearby. When the pasture has run low as seasons change, or trade is no more, they move on. This is partly why Abram and his company travelled in stages.

In their travels, once in a while, they will find a piece of land that topographically is well protected from raids, banditry, and wild animals, is well endowed with pasture and water, and is privately positioned without being too far from trade routes and there they'll pitch tents. Pitching one's tent usually signifies an intention for a longer stay, a more permanent abode. This for Abram at that time was between Bethel and Ai, where he had also erected an altar of faith.

He returned to where he had first pitched his tent, his natural mind was satisfied with his material expansion - indeed he had been blessed- and was ready for a more permanent dwelling. Naturally, we are creatures of habit. His spirit man however had become hungry and thirsty and longed for the presence of the Lord. Upon reaching that place, he called on the Lord by His name; the name that He had had a revelation of in that place a few seasons back. He knew there was more because everything God had promised had not yet come to be. He knew there was more of the God he had first caught a glimpse of, and he wanted to see Him more. This is a liveable example of being content without being complacent or too comfortable.

This part of his journey serves to comfort us. As we are walking with the Lord, there are times when the issues of life overwhelm us and we begin to feel like we have wandered too far away from the Lord. You might attempt to pray but suddenly your petition feels powerless, Bible study feels like hard labour, and generally you can deduce that at some point you stopped walking in God's ordered steps and decided to follow your own lead depending on what you thought life and the situations you are living through demand. The encouragement here is to go back to the place where your tent of meeting with the Lord is, put fire back on the altar, and then remind yourself of the Lord whom you had met there and begin the journey anew.

And I will bless you…

Question.

❖ If God calls you out will you obey? Why or why not?

....

....

....

....

....

<u>Not Everybody can Come.</u>

Genesis 13:5-13

Lot had tents; here is a man who felt satisfied within himself, felt like he had achieved everything worth pursuing and was ready to settle down, make a more permanent abode, and finally cease from moving around so much. To his credit, he had already achieved everything that to a physical eye someone needed to achieve to be seen as prosperous and blessed: he had the wife, children, cattle, gold, servants, and silver. When men of renown in the land stood up he would have been counted among them. Yet there was something that was still cropping up as a contention that would not allow him to relax and enjoy the fruits of his labour. Where they had sojourned in Bethel, the land was occupied by Canaanites and Perizites therefore together with Abram's flock; the pressure on the resources was too high. This caused conflict between their herdsmen, all wanted the flock they tended fed and watered.

Due to this strain and conflict, the time had come for Lot and Abram to part ways and for God's instruction to part from his kindred to be upheld. To avoid further animosity Abram did the wise thing and told Lot to choose which direction he would head into and occupy that land and he would head in the opposite direction. This is an ode to Abram; he surrendered the choice to Lot much as the Lord had already given him the land, for him and his descendants. To Abram it was not so much about the land, but the God who can give land; he chose faith over what the eyes can see, while Lot was satisfied and drew his security from what he could see and touch.

Lot looked around and saw how well-watered the plain of Jordan was, all the way to Zoar. The land was healthy and fertile like the land of Egypt, where they had dwelled previously. He chose to head east into the valley and pitched his tent toward Sodom while Abram remained in the land of Canaan. He looked around and saw a land that would be able to hold all his cattle and souls; to him that plain represented settlement and rest. He looked and saw a goodly land, a place where he could expand his family and possessions, grow old, and die without much struggle. He had become satisfied with all he had achieved and saw no need to go any further with the God whom Abraham had introduced him to. He looked at the land and saw that it was goodly, so it did not matter that the neighbours he would be living next to were wicked and sinners before the Lord. He approved, and did not look deeper to see whether or not the Lord approved. That was as far as his relationship with the God of glory could grow. And so it is with the world right now: righteous men have convinced one another that they can live among the unrighteous, that good and evil can coexist, that you can pray for strength to continue fostering corruption, and as we see as we continue to read on eventually evil

will overwhelm good; you cannot domesticate demons
and then expect your house to still be peaceful.

Questions.

❖ What do you think was the real cause of the
strife between Lot and Abram's herdsmen?

....

....

....

....

❖ What emotions do you suppose Abram felt
when he proposed their separation, and after
their separation?

....

....

....

❖ Do you trust God to lead you even when you
don't know the destination?

....

....

....

...Unto A Land That I Will Shew Thee.

Genesis 13:14-18

Discovering God's will for your life is progressive; first you see the good, then the acceptable, then the perfect will of God (Romans 12:1, 2). It all begins with surrender, give all of you to Him and then as you learn more and more of Him; how He thinks, how He speaks, how He acts, your transformation is made more sure and God's will becomes more and more apparent to you. In Genesis 12, the Lord told Abram that He would give the land to his seed, after he parted ways with Lot, God added another clause to it: *"Lift up now thine eyes, and look from the place where thou art northward, and southward, and eastward, and westward: for all **the land which thou seest, to thee will I give it, and to thy seed forever."(13:14, 15)* .He extended the promise to cover Abram, and all his descendants forever.

When there was strife between Lot and Abram, God was quiet. The Spirit of God is polite; He doesn't give an opinion where it has not been requested. He was watching, to see whether Abram would respond in faith, it was a lesson and he graduated basing on his response. So He could see that there was a man who could be trusted with God's best, and He promoted him. Apart from the land, He also promised that his seed would grow into a multitude that could not be numbered; the Lord was insisting on one of His promises to him of making him a great nation. The Lord also said to Abram "Arise", *'Go and survey the land, walk through it, for I will give it to you'*. The Lord had instructed him to go and survey the land that he and his seed would live on. Since he did not yet have any children, and he was living as a stranger among the Canaanites, Abram could only walk and claim the land by faith. That he did.

So Abram took down his tent and went and dwelt in the plain of Mamre, in Hebron. There he built an altar unto the Lord; an **altar of eternal covenant.** Where a covenant is established and received by faith, thanksgiving becomes a natural successor. You see, thanksgiving is an act of faith, anytime God speaks something over your life in covenant thanksgiving is what you do to say *"Lord I don't see it yet, but I know it is because you have said so."* From then on, his neighbours called him Abram of He'bron, Abram the He'brew man. While Lot had looked up and chosen a place of settlement for himself, Abram had waited on the Lord to tell him to look up and see what He had chosen for him. Faith is demonstrated most when all that is happening in the natural seems to be disadvantageous.

Questions.

❖ What do you think inspired Abram to walk in obedience to the Lord?

....

....

....

....

❖ What are the lessons that you have gleaned so far?..

....

....

....

....

....

Warfare.

Genesis 14

In this study, we're going to explore a war of kings that Abram got involved in as a matter of necessity. Physical wars, for resources, power, and influence were as common 6000 years ago as they are now; what has changed are the scale, number of people involved, and weaponry. There are two things I would like to highlight before we get into the study: firstly, although Abram had been promised by God the land, it wasn't his yet, he still lived among nations with their people and kings. Secondly, in physical warfare much like spiritual warfare, strength, rank and the number of people fighting on your side determine the victory.

There were seven different parties involved in this war. The first group was made up of four kingdoms and their kings, with Chedorlaomer king of Elam as their principal head (prince). They attacked and subdued the second group made up of five nations and their kings. The second group's princes were the kings of Sodom and Gomorrah. The second alliance ended up serving the first for twelve years after their defeat but in the thirteenth year, they rebelled. Rebellion is usually inspired by a people being convinced that they are strong enough to beat their oppressors (rulers).

Chedorlaomer and his alliance decided to go ahead to attack and subdue other kings, to grow their armies and might before dealing with the rebels. They attacked the third group; the Rephaims, Zuzims, Emims, and the Horites, against whom they won. They then went on to attack the fourth group; the Amalekites and the Amorites.

After this, the second alliance went out to battle in the vale of Siddim, where they had fought the first time.

The battle was sore and those led by Chedorlaomer won and the kings of Sodom and Gomorrah fled and fell in the slime pits. The rest of their companies fled into the mountains. The strongmen were beaten and the rest of the army fled. After that, the first alliance plundered the goods of Sodom and Gomorrah and went their way. I hope you remember that Lot had moved to the plains of Sodom right? He was caught up in the plunder and carried away, with all he had.

One person however escaped and carried the news to Abram the Hebrew. The name of Abram had become great in the land, a man and his household who arrived in the land had grown to become a tribe, the Hebrews, and Abram was recognised as their prince. He together with Aner, Eshcol, and Mamre formed the fifth group. They took up arms and pursued the first party to Dan, where they ambushed them at night and pursued them to Damascus. They won and plundered the enemy. He took back everything they had taken from Sodom and Gomorrah including his nephew Lot and his household. After the news of the slaughter of Chedorlaomer spread, the king of Sodom went out to meet him. We are then introduced to the sixth and seventh parties; Melchizedek the king of Salem, and the Most High

God. Melchizedek was both the king of Salem and the priest of the Most High God.

Melchizedek came to meet Abram when he returned from battle, offered him bread and wine and blessed him in the name of the Most High God, and blessed the name of God Most High for Abram's sake, for giving him victory. Here he met a man who had a greater revelation of God, and was more spiritually accomplished than himself. In the pagan world, there was a great king who was both king and priest of the Most High. Only the greater can bless the lesser, and only a superior can offer bread and wine, because bread is the revelation of God and wine is spiritual fortification and strength. Abram gave him a tithe of all their takings; in honour of his office and also in honour of the Most High that he had met through this priest of the Lord. We are introduced to the office of the priesthood, one who is both king and priest. The first communion bread and wine and the first tithe in God's dealings with man were offered on that day. In the natural world, Melchizedek was the mightiest king in the land, because tribute is paid only to the strongest and in the spiritual a priest.

After this, the king of Sodom asked Abram to return his people but keep the property recovered but Abram declined, only claiming what was due to his companions. By the laws of war, both physical and spiritual, the spoils belong to the victor. So all the substance and the people were Abram's by right, but the king of Sodom was in a way asking him to do him a favour. *"But Abram said to the king of Sodom, 'I have raised my hand in an oath to the Lord, God Most High, Creator of heaven and earth, that I will not take a thread or sandal strap or anything that belongs to you, **so you can never say, 'I made Abram rich.'"***(14:22, 23)* Abram could have taken this as a sign that God was indeed blessing him and would have taken it but he had just had an encounter with God and a revelation of another dimension of Him. The condition of his heart is made even more apparent here, because only a man who is totally surrendered to God would have such a high level of discernment. His reason was simple: *"I will not take anything that is thine, lest thou shouldst say, I have made Abram rich."* In his communion with the priest of God Most High, the revelation of God being his source of all good things such as riches and honour had been affirmed.

Questions.

❖ Who among the seven different parties had the greatest army?

....

....

....

....

❖ Why do you think Melchizedek said "Abram of the Most High God"?

....

. . . .

. . . .

. . . .

❖ What is the spiritual significance of paying tithe? Do you practice it?

. . . .

. . . .

. . . .

. . . .

. . . .

<u>Fear Not.</u>

Genesis 15:1

After the war and the decided victory for the ones who fought with God on their side, the word of the Lord came unto Abram in a vision and said to him. *"Fear not Abram: I am thy **shield, and thy exceeding great reward." (15:1)*

Fear not- Do not be afraid, do not worry about the dangers that surround you, do not be anxious for the possibility of another attack on you and yours, and let not your heart be troubled for your safety.

I am thy shield- I will protect you, I will guard you, I have planted myself between you and all your enemies, I am the wall that holds back all who match against you.

Thy exceeding great reward- and I am your ultimate prize, I am your greatest inheritance and for each battle that I win on your behalf the reward, the spoil will be exceedingly much.

When Abram said *"lest thou shouldest say, I have made Abram rich"*, it was a declaration of faithfulness and God honoured His proclamation, He will never let His righteous ones know shame.

❖ Write a declaration of your faith here...
....
....
....
....
....
....
....
....
....

Lord, I have A Question…

Genesis 15:2-21

We're let in on a conversation between God and a man. Abram had a question for the Lord, *"Lord God, what wilt thou give me, seeing I go childless?"* He then went on to tell God about his thought process, in his mind since he did not have his own child, Eliezer, the man who was born to one of his servants and had grown in faithfulness to be the manager of his household would be his heir. To Abram's human mind, he was old and therefore had no hopes of having a child of his own, but he presented that fear to the Lord and waited patiently for God to answer his concern. Never conclude on a matter on your own, present it to the Lord and then wait for Him to teach you how to think about it.

The Lord answered by telling him that he would have a son, out of his bowels. He took him outside in the vision showed him the stars, and told him that his children would be as many as the stars in the sky. The Lord took him outside and said to him, '*If you can be able to count the stars, tell them their sum and call them by name, then you would also be able to number the people that will come forth from you*'. And he said that he would give him seed from his bowels, not his loins. Anything that proceeds from the bowels is a result of faith, because when we labour in prayer and faith, the Bible always associates it with the bowels. So

God was telling him that his faith would bring forth a seed. The word of the Lord says *"And he believed in the Lord, and He counted it to him for righteousness."(15:6)* Abram put his trust in the Lord, and the Lord credited it to him as righteousness. Abram was justified by faith, God was pleased with that. Righteousness is due only to those who walk by faith, not works, not sight. He woke up from this vision, and then continued with his conversation with the Lord; now that he knew God would answer, he got excited, he had tasted and surely the Lord's savour was sweet to the tongue.

God said to him 'I am the Lord who brought you to this land to give it to you as an inheritance'. Abram asked for assurance that he would inherit the land promised to him, the stakes had just gone higher; from possession to inheritance, he had entered the realm of negotiating for generations. The Lord asked him to prepare an animal sacrifice; a three-year-old cow, a three-year-old female goat, a three-year-old ram, a turtledove, and a young bird and offer it to Him as a sacrifice. He however told him not to set it on fire but to just lay it on an altar before the Lord. From the time he slaughtered the animals until evening, Abram stood guard over the sacrifice to make sure the birds of prey did not carry any of it off. Birds of prey are always circling to steal or defile our sacrifices, therefore we must stay alert, to chase them away.

In the evening Abram fell into a deep sleep, the fear of the Lord fell upon him, and in it, the Lord spoke to him. He gave him a view into God's plan for his descendants and the sad and painful parts of the visions sent pain and horror into Abram's heart.

- *Know well that your seed shall be a sojourner in a strange land, where they'll be slaves for four hundred years. When they come out it will be with great wealth.*
- *You shall die in peace in a good old age.*
- *Your seed will inherit all this land, currently occupied by the ten nations, after they return from the land of their oppression in the fourth generation.*

In the dark of the night, a smoking furnace and a burning lamp passed between those pieces of meat; the Lord made a covenant with Abram concerning the land and descendants. God had presented Himself in the covenant as the executor, a party and a witness. Because none is higher than Yahweh, God swore by Himself that He would see the promise to its fulfilment. He reminded Abram that his time on earth would end, but even then the contract would still be valid; it was and eternal covenant.

Questions.

- ❖ What do you think the Lord meant when He said that the iniquity of the Amorites was not yet full?

....

....

....
....
....

❖ Do you have any ideas of birds of prey in your life?

....
....
....
....
....

❖ What is the place of obedience in your relationship with God?

....
....
....
....
....
....

Giving God a Hand.

Genesis 16

When a man truly loves a woman he will do anything for her, even to his own detriment. We see it in Adam and Eve, and again we see it here in Sarai and Abram. Abram must have told Sarai what God had said about him having an heir from his own bowels because soon after Sarai made it her sworn mission to make sure the word came to pass. That she was barren was apparent, but human eyes could not see beyond that fact and that is how far her faith could reach. To bring God's word to pass, she gave her handmaid Hagar to lay with her husband and she got pregnant. The plan according to custom was that Hagar would be more of a surrogate, she would have the baby but it would belong to Sarai and Abram as the parents. However, as soon as she found out she was pregnant; she started acting better than her mistress. So Sarai went to her husband sobbing and was like, *'You don't love me anymore, you love her now that you know her womb works. See, it is your fault my lord that she has the audacity to be rude to me.'* Abram was like, *'My lady, this was your plan, do with her as you please. I only did it to make you happy, I love you.'* So Sarai began being mean and oppressive to Hagar until she ran away because she could not take the suffering anymore. Ten years after Abram moved into Canaan, he had his first recorded marital dispute, and dare I say he handled it well.

The angel of the Lord found her in the wilderness near Shur, and he asked her two questions: where are you from? And where are you going? Sarai's maid could only answer the first question, which she was fleeing from her mistress who was being extremely mean to her. As far as where she was going, she only knew that she was in the general direction of the way that led back to Egypt. The angel told her to go back and submit to her mistress, and attached to that instruction was a promise. The Lord promised to multiply her seed exceedingly beyond numbering; she became the first matriarch in all of Biblical history. Before she left, the angel told her that she would bear a son and name him Ishmael, meaning the Lord hears. He would be a wild man who would fight with everybody and would live among all his brethren.

During that encounter, Hagar had a revelation of God and she called Him *El-Roi, "the one who sees"* for she had seen the Lord who saw and looked after her, the one who saw her through her suffering and affliction, and counted her tears when she cried. She named the well by which she had rested in the wilderness Beerlahairoi meaning *A Well of the Living One Who Sees Me.*

Nobody encounters God and remains the same, Hagar believed and obeyed, and in that act secured her future, her son's future, and all their future generations. Out of her, a nation was born.

❖ Where was the disconnect between God's promise of a child and Sarai's understanding?

....

....

....

....

....

❖ Why do you think Hagar began to despise her mistress?

....

....

....

❖ Have you ever had an encounter in your life that resulted in you having a particular revelation of God's character?

....

....

....

....

Be Thou Perfect- The Covenant, the Circumcision.

Most Bible scholars argue that covenants between God and man are unilateral but I disagree because man always has/had the option of declining to get into agreement with Him. There are also many recorded instances in the Bible where a man got into an agreement with God and still violated the stipulated terms of the agreement. So let us explore the nature of a covenant as a bilateral agreement because it is based on a covenant that any party can lay claim to a promise. A covenant is a testament or a contract between two or more parties where the terms of promises, stipulations, privileges, and responsibilities are laid out, agreed upon, and sealed. After a covenant is ratified or sealed, it cannot be nullified before the time stipulation; it can only be built upon.

Thirteen years passed after the birth of Ishmael, and when Abram was ninety-nine years old the Lord appeared unto him and said *"I am the Almighty God (El Shaddai), **walk before me, and be thou perfect."***(17:1) Being perfect here implies a process of cleansing and sanctification after a perceived disobedience, it is to walk in the right way- the Lord's way- and be blameless. God was also revealing His nature to Abram; He was introducing Himself as a God who takes covenant seriously, and expected the person

He was relating to honour covenant as well. He was also teaching Abram that part of being a friend of God was doing the right thing, never anything that would jeopardise the relationship. At that point I think Abram remembered all the times he had done what was convenient instead of what was right and his face hit the ground in repentance.

El Shaddai told him that if he did this He would make a covenant between them and multiply him exceedingly. Abram threw himself on his face before the Lord, as an act of expressing his perfect heart and pure intentions and the Lord spoke to him further. *"Behold, my covenant is with you, and you shall be the father of a multitude of nations. No longer shall your name be called Abram, but your name shall be Abraham, for I have made you the father of a multitude of nations."(17:14, 15).* That new name would be a daily reminder to Abraham of the promise. The order is God speaks to you, you submit and your heart is renewed and your mind transformed, and then He gives you a new name.

In the covenant, a few more stipulations were added:
- I will make thee exceedingly fruitful (in all ways and all areas of life).
- I will make nations of thee (not just tribes, but independent nations).
- Kings shall come out of thee (rulers and leaders shall be born from you, what are nations without kings?).

- I will establish my covenant between me and thee and thy seed after thee in their generations for an everlasting covenant, to be a God unto thee and thy seed after thee.
- I will give unto thee and unto thy seed after thee, the land wherein thou art a stranger, for a lasting possession.

The Almighty God added a time condition to the covenant; it would be an everlasting covenant - for as long as man and the earth existed, their covenant would remain. The Lord promised to be their God forever and to uphold His part of the covenant on condition that Abraham and his descendants would uphold theirs.

The responsibilities for the covenant on Abraham's side were these:

- He and all his generations would keep it.
- Every man-child among them had to be circumcised at eight days old, as a token seal of the covenant between them.

All the male children, whether part of the family by blood or from servants and slaves were circumcised as a physical marker and reminder to the entire covenant between God and themselves. Any who would not be circumcised would have to be excommunicated.

The Lord also changed Sarai's name to Sarah- meaning mother of nations- and promised that she would bear a son and kings of people would be of her.

All that the Lord had said up to that point made logical sense to Abraham, but when he said Sarah would have a child, Abraham laughed in his heart. In his mind, he contemplated a ninety-year-old woman and a hundred-year-old man having a child together and it seemed impossible. In his natural mind, he already had a son of his bowels, and technically of Sarah's, and so he proclaimed *"O that Ishmael might live before thee!"(17:18)*, oh that Ishmael may live by your favour. God in His foreknowledge and long-suffering told Abraham that He hadn't made a mistake, that indeed Sarah would bear a son and they would name him Isaac- meaning he laughs- Not only would he be the promised child, he would also be the one with whom the covenant would be established forever.

"*But*" the Lord said "*since you have mentioned Ishmael, I blessed him too, I already promised to make him fruitful, and multiply him exceedingly. Now I'm telling you too, he shall beget twelve princes and I shall make him a great nation.*"(17:20) However the Lord insisted to him again that the same time in the coming year Sarah would bear him a son, the promised child who the Lord would maintain the covenant with. After the Lord finished talking and went up, Abraham took Ishmael and all the males in his household and circumcised all of them on the very day that the Lord had said it. Abraham was a changed man, he believed and acted on his faith, his answer was *yes Lord.*

Questions.

* ❖ What was the place of waiting in Abraham's promises?

....

....

....

....

....

❖ Discuss the sovereignty of God as depicted in
this portion of scripture.

....

....

....

....

....

....

Entertaining Angels- Is Anything Too Hard for The Lord?

Genesis 18:1-16

By this time, Abraham had walked with the Lord for twenty-four years. His faith had grown and his ways in the faith had matured; evidenced by the fruit of love, gentleness, and kindness born in his life as demonstrated in the hospitality that he extended to these three men who approached his tent in the heat of the day. Only a person with the love of God in his heart would say to strangers *"I will bring a bit of bread so that you may strengthen yourselves. This is why you have passed your servant's [way]. Later, you can continue." "Yes,"* they replied, *"do as you have said."* (17:5) we express God's love in us by loving those around us and helping those in need. Abraham's thought was the men had passed his way so that he could get an opportunity to serve them.

His tent was still pitched in the plains of Mamre, where he had settled after he and Lot parted ways. If you have ever been in a desert or semi-desert climate for a time then you'll attach a bit more magnitude to the act of kindness Abraham extended to that group. He rushed to them and invited them into his household with the utmost humility. He offered them water to wash the dust and heat off, shade from the scorching sun, and some bread and rest before they could go on with their journey.

After they settled under a tree, Abraham rushed into the tent and asked Sarah to prepare some cakes. He ran and picked out the best calf from his herd and gave it to a young man who slaughtered it and prepared the meat. He then took the food with butter and milk and offered it to them. Like a good host, he stood by to attend them while they ate. Such acts of hospitality are lost to humanity, but in some communities in Africa and Asia, special attention is still paid to guests and ceremonies usually accompany it.

Of the three men, one was the Lord. They asked him *"Where is Sarah thy wife?"(18:9)* to which he answered *"In the tent."* the Lord said *"I will certainly return unto thee according to the time of life; and, lo, Sarah thy wife shall have a son".(18:10)* Sarah was old, and the statement to her sounded preposterous so she laughed within herself. The Lord asked, *"Wherefore did Sarah laugh... Is anything too hard for the Lord?"(18:13, 14).* Is anything too marvellous for the Lord? Is there anything in the universe that God cannot do? And then he reiterated *'in the time it takes a woman to have a baby, Sarah shall bear a son'.* Sarah at that point was afraid and said *'I didn't laugh',* and the Lord interjected *'Well, you did'.* Notice also that Abraham's discernment had grown because when the Lord began to speak he KNEW who it was.

Abraham, like an excellent host, saw them off on their way toward Sodom. Again, this is a practice that is still widely appreciated in Africa, I don't have enough words to describe its significance so I will use one word; HONOUR.

❖ Do you think before this interaction, Sarah knew the Lord?

....
....
....

❖ Make comparisons between the interactions of God with Adam and Eve and Abraham and Sarah, and draw parallels and contrasts.

....
....
....
....
....
....
....
....

❖ Contrast God's interactions with Abraham and Sarah to how He interacts with Christians currently. What brought about the change?

....
....
....
....
....

. . . .

. . . .

. . . .

The Righteous Shall Never Be Forsaken.

Genesis 18:17-33

As Abraham was seeing them off, the Lord began reflecting within Himself, *"Shall I hide from Abraham that thing which I do; Seeing that Abraham <u>shall surely become</u> a great and mighty nation, and all the nations of the earth <u>shall be blessed in him</u>? For <u>I know him</u>, that <u>he will command</u> his children and his household after him, and they shall keep the way of the Lord, to do justice and judgment; <u>that the Lord may bring upon Abraham</u> that which He hath spoken of him."* (18:17-19)

I want to highlight here that the Lord said that it is by Abraham instructing his children and his posterity to keep the way of the Lord, by doing what is just and right that the promises of God to Abraham would come to be. This is the same truth that was made apparent to Joshua in 1:8 as the formula for obtaining prosperity and good success.

The Lord had searched Abraham's heart and approved of his character. He knew him and knew that all that He had promised him would be because Abraham would uphold their covenant. And so He let Abraham in on the secret of Sodom and Gomorrah and the plan He had regarding those two nations.

Abraham stood before the Lord and asked *"Wilt thou also destroy the righteous with the wicked?"*

(18:23) 'If there are fifty righteous in that cruel and sinful city will you spare it for their sake?' - Here Abraham called upon one of His names and therefore attributes *"Shall not the Judge of all the earth do right?"(18:25)* - to which the Lord answered that if there were fifty righteous He would spare it.

I think Abraham knew Sodom and Gomorrah quite well because again he asked *'What if there are forty-five will you spare it?'* to which He answered yes. He again asked *'What if there are only forty?'*, and then thirty, twenty, and finally ten, to which the Lord answered in the affirmative. *"I will not destroy it."*

The two men that were with the Lord had gone ahead into Sodom and Gomorrah. After the conversation was over the Lord went his way and Abraham returned to his tent. We know from Genesis 19 that fire and brimstone rained upon the city from heaven but Lot and his family were saved, those were all the righteous people that the Lord could find in that wicked city.

We are prone to do what Abraham did for Sodom, intercede and negotiate with the Lord for people's lives. Like Abraham, we do it with a very limited view of creation and God's purpose; while we care so much about physical creation and what we can see, God is more invested in souls and their eternal standing. He had looked and seen Sodom was wicked, maybe not all practiced the debauchery, but can two walk together except they be agreed? If you live among drunkards, you must at least believe there is nothing wrong with being a drunk else you would have moved to a different neighbourhood. As the Lord often does with men and women who have His heart, He did Abraham a favour and saved the household of Lot. And here we see that Abraham was primarily concerned about t his nephew. As you read the passage that we will skip over, you discover that Lot's daughters had the mind set of Sodom, and by them the two nations that hated and oppressed Israel in history were born. Abraham in his concern extended an evil into the future and gave it opportunity to be bigger.

Questions.

❖ Do a personal reading of Genesis 19, what have you learned from it?

....

....

....

....

....

....

....

....

....

....

....

......

❖ What is the place of intercession in our lives?

....

. . . .
. . . .
. . . .
. . . .
. . . .
. . . .
. . . .
. . . .
. . . .
. . . .
. . . .
. . . .

The Fear of God is not in this Place...I thought.

Genesis 20

Abraham recognised the end of a season and moved on to Gerar in the south. On arriving there, he did something he had done before in Egypt, he introduced his wife as his sister to all, including King Abimelech. Sarah was still a fine babe at the age of ninety, and the king just had to have her; spiritually we can posit that he looked at her and the deities he worshipped could see she was ripe for birthing and wanted to take that opportunity to interfere with the plans of God. At this point, the Lord could not let Abimelech have her as a wife, because the promised son needed both Abraham and Sarah to be born.

God appeared to Abimelech in a dream and put His fear in him, telling him *"Thou art a dead man, for the woman whom thou hast taken..."* We continue to see God here as Judge as we had been introduced to us earlier. Abimelech, however, had not touched her nor had he taken her knowing she was somebody's wife, therefore, he said *"Lord, wilt thou slay also a righteous nation?"* and went on to explain that Abraham and Sarah had deceived him knowingly. He called on the Lord as one who judges righteously and looks at the hearts of men. The Lord told Abimelech that he had purposely come to stop him from sinning and asked him to give Abraham his wife back, and Abraham who was a prophet would pray for him and he would live and not die. The king rose early and went to do what the Lord had commanded. He questioned Abraham who replied, *"Because I thought, Surely the fear of God is not in this place; and they will slay me for my wife's sake."* And then he added, *'Technically she's my sister, my half-sister.'*

So Abimelech, intending to receive a prophet's reward did unto Abraham an honour befitting a prophet; he took sheep, oxen, menservants, and maidservants and gave them unto Abraham, together with Sarah his wife. He extended an invitation to Abraham to dwell wherever he pleased in his kingdom and paid one thousand pieces of silver to Abraham as a fine for his wrongdoing and to declare Sarah's innocence and restore her honour. Forgiveness was sought and found between the parties. The Lord had shut all the wombs in Abimelech's house when he took Sarah. So Abraham prayed for him and God healed Abimelech, his wife, and his maid servants and they became fruitful once more. Through Abraham, a nation had been blessed.

Questions.

❖ What do you understand by "the fear of God"?

....

....

....

....

✦ What is the trait in Sarah that her attractive to kings?

✦ What do you understand from what Abraham said to Abimelech to explain his deception?

At The Set Time.

According to His promise the Lord did unto Sarah, she conceived and bore Abraham a son *"at the set time of which God had spoken to him"*. The boy was named Isaac by his father and on the eighth day, Abraham circumcised him as the Lord commanded.

Abraham was one hundred years old when his son was born; twenty-five years after God had called Abraham forth from Ur of the Chaldees.

Sarah was well pleased and said, *"God hath made me to laugh so that all that hear will laugh with me."* When the child was weaned, Abraham hosted a great feast to celebrate!

Questions.

❖ What do you understand about times and seasons in relation to God's promises?

....

....

....

....

....

....

Because He Is Thy Seed.

Genesis 21:9-21

Sarah expected people to laugh with her- celebrating and congratulating- but Ishmael laughed -mocking- and that angered her. She went to her husband and demanded that Hagar, who was a slave, and her son be run out of their household because a slave's son could not be a co-heir with her son. Abraham was sad because Ishmael was also his son. The Lord however told Abraham to listen to his wife because *"In Isaac shall thy seed be called."* He also promised to make Ishmael a nation *"because he is thy seed"*. Abraham, his heart at peace, rose early took food and a bottle of water gave it to Hagar, and sent them away.

Hagar left and wandered in the wilderness of Beersheba. In a while, the water ran out and in a desert that spelled death. She set her son under a shrub and went a bowshot distance off, sat down, and began to weep. The Lord who saw her followed His word and sent an angel to their aid. The angel called at her from heaven *"Fear not; for God hath heard the voice of the lad where he is."* Hagar was the one sobbing but in heaven the Lord heard it as Ishmael needing His help. Because of the promise the Lord had made to Abraham concerning Ishmael, his life was preserved.

God opened Hagar's eyes and she saw a well of water, she filled the bottle and gave the lad to drink. Here is a picture of a God who waters His flock even in dry lands. God was with the lad and he grew and dwelt in the wilderness of Paran and became an archer. His mother brought him a wife out of the land of Egypt.

Question

- ❖ Why was Ishmael mocking Sarah?

....

....

....

....

A Covenant with God As The Witness.

Genesis 21:22-34

When we make agreements/covenants with each other, with God as the witness, He becomes the upholder, sustainer, and executor of the consequences should any party breach it. That is why the marriage covenant is sacred and should not be broken.

King Abimelech and his chief captain Phichol went to speak with Abraham. They had seen that God was with him in all that he did so he said *"Now **therefore** swear unto me here **by God** that thou wilt not deal falsely with me, nor with thy son, nor with thy son's son: but according to the kindness that I have done unto thee, thou shalt do unto me, and to the land wherein thou hast sojourned."* And Abraham said, **"I swear."**

Note that firstly, Abimelech was convinced that in a fight between him and Abraham, Abraham would win because God would fight on his side. Secondly, he still had a memory of Abraham being deceptive. Thirdly, the covenant was to the third generation, anything either of the descendants did after that would not be in breach. Fourthly, there cannot be a covenant without forgiveness and reconciliation on both sides, both would not have honoured it if there were strife: hence the restoration of the well at Beersheba and the exchange of the seven ewe lambs to mark it. And finally, the land was included in the covenant; because the earth bears the brunt of war and keeps records of all transactions among human beings. Abimelech accepted the seven ewe lambs from Abraham as a sign that he was the one who dug the well at Beersheba.

A sign and seal of the covenant were performed when Abraham took sheep and oxen and gave them to Abimelech. We value things and people for which we have paid a cost; the more we've given the higher the perceived value. In the previous chapter, Abimelech gifted Abraham, but in this chapter the opposite, because while Abraham was prophet, Abimelech was still king over that land, we give honour to whom it is due.

After this, Abimelech and Phichol rose and went back into the land of the Philistines. Abraham then planted a grove and called there on the name of the Lord the everlasting God. The moment Abimelech restored the well back to Abraham he dedicated it to the Lord, planted trees around it, and made it a place of worship to the Everlasting God. The agreement would last to the third generation, but Jehovah would be the Lord over that land forever. Abraham sojourned in the Philistine's land for many days.

Questions.

❖ Why do you think Abimelech saw the need for a formal agreement?

....

....

....

....

....

❖ Is there a parallel between their style of making agreements and ours presently?

....

....

....

....

A test- Jehovah-Jireh.

Genesis 22

A few years passed, one day God called Abraham and he said *"Here I am."* The Lord said unto him to take his favoured son Isaac into the land of Moriah and offer him as a burnt sacrifice upon one of the mountains on one of the peaks that He would show him. Abraham rose early the next morning, saddled his ass, took his son Isaac, wood for the burnt offering, and two of his young men, and on they went. They arrived after a three-day journey and Abraham told his young men to wait at a far-off location while he went up with his son to worship. The three day march must have been solemn, but the climb up the mountain must have been even tenser.

He took the wood and gave it to Isaac to carry because he was old obviously. Isaac had a question, *"Behold the fire and the wood: but where is the lamb for a burnt offering?"* Abraham's answer was off-tense but on-point! *"God will provide Himself a lamb for a burnt offering".* When they got to the place, Abraham built an altar, laid out the wood, and then bound Isaac and laid him on the altar. He then raised his knife ready to kill his son.

An angel of the Lord called him from heaven and told him not to kill his son *"for now I know that thou fearest God."* When Abraham looked around, there was a ram caught in the thicket by its horns. He took the ram and offered him as a burnt offering instead of his son. Here we get an introduction to the substitutionary offering. *"Abraham called the name of that place Jehovah- Jireh, as it is said to this day, In the mount of the Lord it shall be seen."* The generous hand of the Lord was seen on that day.

Isaac was a young man, old enough to carry firewood, old enough to walk for three days to go and worship. He could have resisted his old father when he bound him and placed him on the altar but he did not. In fact, he might have climbed up on the altar himself and laid still as his father bound him to it. He helped his father put the stones together to build the altar. He was the first person to ever surrender his body as living sacrifice! El Sahddai became the Fear of Isaac on that altar; he discovered the perfect will of God on that day. Abraham on the other hand- dear old faithful Abraham- he was willing to watch his only hope in this entire world die, he did not mind breaking his heart when he plunged the knife into his sons; he was ready to give up his only son. And Paul tells us something even more glorious about this: our father Abraham was doing it in joy knowing that God was also able to raise his son back from the dead (Hebrews 11:19). .

On the mount of the Lord, there is vision; Abraham had received the revelation of the Lord who provides. The angel again called out of heaven and said to Abraham, seeing you were ready to offer your son as a burnt offering, *"In blessing, I will bless thee, and in multiplying I will multiply thy seed as the stars of heaven, and as the sand which is upon the seashore; and thy seed shall possess the gates of his enemies. And in thy seed shall all the nations of the earth be blessed; because thou hast obeyed my voice."*

The Lord added another provision to their covenant; He promised to make people fear Abraham, he would be the terror that possesses the gates of his enemies. Men would either bless themselves through him, or be cursed through him, the choice was with the people, but the verdict was with the Lord. Abraham and Isaac returned to the young men and together they went back to their tents at Beersheba. On that day, the Almighty Everlasting God and Judge of Abraham became the Fear of Isaac. What's more, our Lord Jesus and salvation and adoption were promised to us.

While he was dwelling there, he received a good report of how his brother Nahor's family had grown.

Questions.

❖ Why did Abraham rise early?

....

....

....

....

....

❖ In your view, how was Abraham able to bind up Isaac despite him being a young man and his father an old one?

....

....

....

....

❖ Was it lying when Abraham told Isaac "God will provide"?

....

....

....

❖ How do you involve your children in worship and fellowship?

....

....

....

....

A Death, a Burying Place.

At the ripe age of 127 years, Sarah died and Abraham mourned her. During their period of staying in that land, they were technically strangers and sojourners- to bring it closer to home, approved squatters or resident foreigners- so when Abraham needed to bury Sarah he thought it should be on land that he possessed.

He spoke to the sons of Heth about his possible owning of a burying plot. He asked them to talk to Ephron, the son of Zohar, to sell him a plot of land that had a cave in it. The landowners told him that since he was a prince, the chosen one of the Lord among them, he could bury his dead wherever he pleased. They said that they would give it to him to bury his dead, in present terms they were saying:' *you can take it, but you owe me'*. Had Abraham agreed to the deal, Heth and all the Hittites would have something to hold over his head. He however insisted on buying a burial cave. So they did, and Ephron agreed, but he wanted to give it to Abraham for free together with the land and trees surrounding the cave. Abraham however insisted on paying for its true value, which was four hundred shekels of silver. In those days, writing wasn't commonplace; contracts were considered valid and executable when an agreement was reached between parties in front of witnesses. For something as important as the sale of land, it was done in the presence of elders. The transaction was certified at the gate, where all important legal matters would be attended to in olden times.

It took plenty of humility for Abraham to bow down before the elders of the land, almost pleading with them to sell him a cave as a burial place. He was bowing down to beg to buy a minute portion of the land that the Lord had bequeathed to him and his descendants forever. In that moment, it was also a declaration by him that indeed he had left Mesopotamia behind, that even in death he belonged and laid claim to Canaan. It is amazing really that one of the postures of expressing humility before God and man is being down on the earth on your knees, your face, or even fully prostrated.

I would like to add as a side note that the value of things has always been dependent on trade, Abraham weighed out silver according to the weights of the merchants. Another point on this is money is important to have while living on earth, as a tool of trade, a measure of value, and a store of riches. Do not worship money, but do not underestimate its place in the life of subduing and having dominion here on earth.

So it was, and Abraham came into possession of the field of Ephron which was in Machpelah, *"the field and the cave which was therein, and all the trees that were in the field, that were in all the borders roundabout were made sure."* They even counted the trees. They all walked around the land, marked the boundaries and made it sure in front of withnesses, and the transaction was recorded. After that, Abraham buried Sarah in the cave.

❖ What does this passage teach you about money?

....

....

....

....

❖ Why is Abraham 'bowing' greatly emphasised in this passage?

....

....

....

....

❖ Why was it important for Abraham to own the land?

....

....

....

....

<u>Blessed In All Things.</u>

Genesis 24:1

"And Abraham was old, and well stricken in age: and THE LORD HAD BLESSED ABRAHAM IN ALL THINGS. " He who could only swear by Himself had promised, of course it happened. Abraham was content, he had entered rest.

Questions.

❖ What were the blessings that Abraham had experienced in his walk with the Lord?

....

....

....

....

....

....

....

....

....

....

❖ Would you say that all of God's promises to Abraham had been fulfilled?

....

....

....

....

69

....
....
....
....
....
....
....
....

A Command Given, and A Prayer Answered.

Genesis 24:2-21

The old man had one last thing he needed to do, getting his son a bride; his offspring was important to the whole of humanity after all.

Abraham made his eldest servant swear by *"the Lord, the God of heaven, and the God of earth"* to go back to his country and his kindred, to take a wife for his son Isaac. He was adamant about him not marrying a Canaanite woman- when you marry someone, you marry their family, practices, cultures, beliefs, and even God(gods)- The servant had a concern, that if he found a girl but she refused to accompany him, could he bring Isaac to Mesopotamia, to which Abraham answered *"NO!"* He told his servant that the Lord God whom he served would send his angel before him to ensure that Isaac would have the wife, and if not then the servant would be free from the vow.

The servant put his hand under Abraham's thigh and swore by the God of heaven and the God of the earth - the one who in Genesis 1:1 created heaven and the earth. Remember in the previous text when Abraham had thought that the fear of God was not in a land? He had now come to the revelation of the Might and the Omnipresence of God- to carry out his mission. I would like to take you farther into the book of Genesis to when Jacob wrestled all night with an angel and he said

"I will not let thee go unless thou bless me", the angel touched Jacob's thigh when he blessed him. (Genesis 32:24-30) Customarily, in those days swearing by touching the thigh implied that if the oath were not fulfilled in a lifetime then future generations would take on the responsibility of upholding or fulfilling the oath depending on which side they were on.

The servant was in charge of all of Abraham's possessions, so he took ten camels laden with gifts and departed into Mesopotamia, Nahor's city. He let his camels kneel by a well of water, in the evening, when women went out to draw. And then he prayed… *"O Lord God of my master Abraham, I pray thee, send me good speed this day, and show kindness unto my master Abraham… And let it come to pass that the damsel to whom I shall say, Let down thy pitcher, I pray thee, that I may drink, and she shall say Drink, and I will give thy camels drink also; let the same be she that thou has appointed for thy servant Isaac; and thereby shall I know that thou hast shewed kindness unto my master."* And he prayed, *'Let her be the one that You Lord have chosen for my master Isaac.'*

Shortly after he finished, Rebekah, Bethuel's daughter, and Nahor's granddaughter came out with her pitcher on her shoulder. She was beautiful and a virgin (like the bride of Christ). When she came from the well, the servant ran to her and asked for water and she said *"Drink my lord"*. When he was sated she also offered to water his camels. A camel can drink up to 150 litres of water at once; drawing up to 1500 litres of water from a well isn't an easy feat is it? She was a strong woman. The man waited patiently and in silence, to see whether or not the Lord had made his journey successful. The Lord had answered his prayer, but was it according to the particular request of his master?

Questions.

❖ Why did Abraham insist that Isaac should marry from his kindred?

....
....
....
....
....

❖ Why was Abraham adamant about Isaac never going back to the land of his kindred?

....
....
....
....

❖ What inspired Rebekah's act of kindness?

....
....
....

❖ Discuss how Abraham's trusted servant could be a type of the Holy Spirit.

....
....
....

. . . .
. . . .
. . . .
. . . .
. . . .
. . . .
. . . .
. . . .
. . . .
. . . .
. . . .

<u>The Lord Led Me.</u>

After the camels were watered, the man gave
Rebekah a golden earring of half a shekel and two
bracelets of ten shekels of gold. He then asked her
whose daughter she was and whether he could find
lodging at their home; there was still the task of finding
out whether she was of the house of Abraham's kin
*"Bethuel's daughter, whose Milcah's son born to
Nahor"*, she answered. He knew then she fulfilled two
of the three requirements; he was hopeful and excited.
She then added that they had feed for the camels and
lodgings. The Lord had exceeded his expectations;
overwhelmed, he bowed down and worshipped the
Lord… *"Blessed be the Lord God of my master
Abraham, who hath not left destitute my master of his
mercy and his truth; I being in the way, the Lord led me
to the house of my master's brethren."* The servant
knelt down and thanked the Lord for hearing him and
coming to his aid for his master's sake. He marvelled at
the kind of loyalty and faithfulness both the Lord and
Abraham exhibited in their love for each other.

I imagine that Rebekah ran home with her pitcher
empty and told her family these things. If it were my
mom, the first question she would ask would be *'I sent
you for water, where is it'* When Laban her brother
heard her story and saw her ornaments, he ran to the
well to meet this strange man. He invited him to their

dwellings as *"blessed of the Lord"*. That became the point of association for them, they both knew the Lord. In this divided and divisive world- race, country, continent, economic regions and trade zones, special groups, gender, and religion- we should always remember that Jesus Christ when interceding for us in heaven introduces us as brethren before the Father. All points of division are unimportant, Christ makes us all one.

The man went into their house, attended to his camels and he and the men that were under him washed their feet. Food was offered to them but he insisted that he wouldn't eat until he told them why he was there. He was told to speak on…

Questions.

❖ What is the significance of them washing their feet?

....
....
....
....
....

❖ What is the significance of him bowing to worship?

....
....
....
....

....

....

....

❖ Why do you think Rebekah ran off to tell those of her mother's house about the man?

....

....

....

....

....

❖ Why was a man given such an important task but his name was not mentioned even once?

....

....

....

....

....

The Pitch- The Testimony.

Genesis 24:34-49

He began by saying *"I am Abraham's servant"*, of course, they knew who Abraham was. He also gave a short account of Abraham's life since he left his country, father's house, and kindred. He told them how the Lord had blessed his master greatly and had made him a great man; he owned a lot of flocks, herds, silver, gold, menservants and maidservants, camels, and asses. How he had an only son to whom he had given all that he had. It is the blessing of the Lord that makes us rich.

He told them his errand and the promise he had made to Abraham about a wife for his son. He told them of the assurance that Abraham had of God, whose ways he followed, sending an angel before his servant to make his mission a success and facilitate him bringing a wife for Isaac from his father's house. We see here again the beauty of free will and choice; Abraham was certain that the Lord would go before his servant and lead him to his kin in Mesopotamia because this was at the Lord's counsel, but whether or not they would let their daughter go was still in their power. Lastly, he gave an account of his prayer to the Lord and how he believed it had been answered by his encounter with Rebekah.

When he had finished his narration, he then requested them to give him an answer to his request of

taking Rebekah as a wife for Isaac. He added that if
they would say no, he would keep looking.

❖ What is the place of testimony in a believer's
life?

....
....
....
....
....

❖ What is prayer to you? Do you know how to
pray?

....
....
....
....

❖ Can you say with confidence that God answers
prayer?

....
....
....
....
....

A Bride for Isaac.

"Laban and Bethuel answered and said, this thing proceedeth from the Lord: we cannot speak unto thee bad or good." (24:50) They told him they agreed and would heed as the Lord had spoken. When he heard what they said, he bowed and worshipped the Lord.

The servant then brought forth jewels of silver and gold and fine clothes and gave them to Rebekah, he also gave precious things to her brother and mother. They then ate and drank and spent the night there. In the morning he wanted to leave but Laban and Milcah said that they should stay for ten days. He insisted that they should send him away, so they called Rebekah to ask her whether she would leave with them and she agreed. Her father's household blessed her and sent her away with her nurse. The blessing was as follows:*" Be the mother of thousands of millions, and let thy seed possess the gate of those which hate them."* The blessings of Rebekah's family to her were similar to God's blessings over Isaac.

Isaac had just come back from Beer-lahai-roi, the well where El-Roi had met with Hagar. He had gone out in the fields to meditate and saw the camels coming. When Rebekah saw Isaac, she alighted from the camel and veiled herself. The bride was clothed in linen, which is the righteous works of the saints. (Revelation 19:8) Every good work- action in response to faith, which is cultivated by following in His ways-, adds a thread to the fine linen we will be dressed in as the bride of Christ. Rebekah had believed and from that faith had left her kin, her land, and her father's house for the promise of a husband in a far-off land whom the Lord had ordained purpose over his life.

The servant gave Isaac an account of his journey. Isaac took Rebekah to his mother's tent and made his betrothed his wife, so he was comforted after the death of his mother.

Questions.

❖ Draw parallels between Isaac and Christ.

....
....
....
....
....
....
....
....
....
....
....
....
....
....

❖ Why did Rebekah veil herself?

....

....

....

....

....

❖ Why do you think Rebekah said, "I will go"?

....

....

....

....

Abraham Is Gathered Up.

Abraham took another wife named Keturah, who bore him six sons. To these, he gave gifts and sent them away when they came of age, into the east country but he willed everything he owned to Isaac. At the good old age of 175 years, Abraham gave up the ghost and was gathered to his people. *"He took his last breath and died at a ripe old age, old and contented, and he was gathered to his people."* He lived a long, productive, and peaceful life. On his deathbed, he was at peace, content, because he had arranged all his worldly affairs and there would be no strife among his children after he was gone. He also had the assurance from God that he would be gathered to his fathers in peace and would be buried honourably.

Isaac and Ishmael buried him in the cave at Machpelah where Sarah was buried. Now we await the resurrection of the saints.

Questions.

❖ Up to this point, had all of God's promises to Abraham been fulfilled?

....

....

....

....

❖ Who were the descendants of Abraham's sons
   by Keturah

....
....
....
....
....
....
....

❖ What is the time between the promise and its
   fulfillment?

....
....
....
....
....
....
....
....
....

Part 2: The Fulfilment of God's Promises to Abraham.

The Appropriation Principle.

Some truths in the Bible are foundational to our relationship with God: firstly, God does not change, so any changes that need to be for us to relate with Him better are on our side, secondly, God is perfectly just, so He is not a respecter of persons, thirdly, God is perfect, we, on the other hand, are not, so the work of us being perfected is inspired, worked in and concluded by the Spirit of God working in us, and fourthly a relationship with God is not based on feeling or intuition, but on principles, promises, and covenants. Our role in it is believing, obeying, and being faithful as He is faithful.

In the story of Abraham that we have studied so far, all these come out clearly in how God walked with Abraham in his faith journey with the Lord being constant, unchanging, all-wise, all-knowing, and long-suffering. Abraham went through a journey of renewing his mind; with the first step of obedience he took being him presenting his body as a living sacrifice (Romans 12:1-3). In agreeing to leave his place of safety he was in effect surrendering first his earthly vessel to the Lord's service. There is also an important principle demonstrated here, of the patriarch (head) of the household/ family believing to the salvation of his entire household- are there any neo-feminists here?- It was so in the days of Noah, it was replicated in the life of Jacob and Joshua, among many other patriarchs; including Joseph, Jesus' earthly father.

We all know that when one believes in their heart and confesses with their tongue that Jesus Christ is the Son of God then salvation is attained. One is at that point born again, a new man is formed in them who is spirit and can relate with the Spirit of God. The Passover lamb has been slaughtered, but the dipping of the hyssop and transferring the blood from the basin to the doorposts is what offered salvation- the tongue, in this case, is the hyssop, by confessing one expresses that *'Jesus Christ didn't just die (historical and theological fact), but He died for ME.'* (Revelation 12:10, 11) It is the confession and testimony that silences the devil (Psalm 8, Matthew 21:16).

In that way, the second and third parts of this book will be drawing a line from Abraham the patriarch of the Hebrew nation to us the Church and God's new creation in Jesus Christ, and how the blessings of Abraham are due to us as much as we're not all his seed biologically, and how to appropriate them so that they can be made manifest in our lives and so that we can be it experientially.

Questions

❖ Looking at Israel right now, would you say they are living in God's promises?

....

....

....

....

....
....
....
....
....
....

God's Promises to Abraham.

We have seen that God's promises to Abraham are what we understand today as contractual agreements. They had elements of bilateral contracts because each party was both a promisor and the promised. The other elements were law and witnesses, and God was both: *"For when God made a promise to Abraham because He could swear by no greater, He sware by Himself."* (Hebrews 6:13). Abraham was the promisor and the promised; *"And so after he had patiently endured, he obtained the promise." (Hebrews 6:15)*

We will venture to hereon reiterate God's promises to Abraham and then later explore how they were fulfilled.

GENESIS 12:1-3	
GOD	**ABRAHAM**
1. To make Abraham a great nation. 2. To bless him and make his name great. 3. To make him a blessing. 4. He will bless those who bless him and curse him who curse him. 5. In Abraham shall all	To leave his country, his kindred, and his father's house, and to go and follow the Lord where He leads.

the families of the world be blessed.	

<u>GENESIS 13:14-17</u>

GOD	ABRAHAM
1. To give Abraham and his seed the land he was in forever. 2. To multiply his seed as the dust of the earth.	Separated himself from his kin Lot.

<u>GENESIS 14:19 - 15:21</u>

GOD	ABRAHAM
1. Promised to be his shield (protector)and his prosperer. 2. That He would give Abraham an heir, of his own blood. 3. To give him seed as the stars. 4. That Abraham's seed shall be strangers and slaves in a foreign land for 400 years but that He would lead them back to	1. Gave tithes to Melchizedek the priest of the Most High God. 2. Refused to take goods of the hands of the king of Sodom in the name of the Lord.

their promised inheritance. 5. That Abraham would live a long life and shall die in peace. 6. He had given to Abraham's seed the land from the River of Egypt to the River Euphrates.	

<u>GENESIS 17:5-11</u>

GOD	ABRAHAM
1. To make him a father of many nations. 2. He would be a God unto him and to his seed forever. 3. Give to Abraham's seed possession and be their God.	1. All the males in his home are to be circumcised as a token forever. 2. To keep the covenant.

<u>GENESIS 22:12-18</u>

GOD	ABRAHAM
1. In blessing, He would bless him. 2. In multiplying He would multiply his	1. Withheld not his only son but was ready to offer him to God as a

seeds as the stars and as the sand upon the seashore. 3. Abraham's seed shall possess the gates of his enemies. 4. In his seed shall all the nations of the earth be blessed.	burnt offering. (He obeyed God's voice).

Questions.

❖ A few of the promises were repeated in recurring passages, why do you think it was so?

....

....

❖ Which of these promises predicted the birth of the Messiah?

....

....

....

❖ What do you understand by 'righteousness' as attributed to Abraham?

....

....

....

How The Promises Were Fulfilled to Abraham.

Make Abraham a great nation.

Abraham was blessed and made a great nation in his lifetime and after. As early as Genesis 16 we see that he was already considered as one among the mighty princes in the land where he lived. In his time he defeated five kings in battle, had much cattle, herds, and servants, and had wonderful relationships with the kings of the lands in which he dwelled.

After his death, God continued to bless the Hebrews and when He delivered them from Egypt He made them a great nation. A small people at first, they conquered many nations and grew in numbers and wealth steadily as they were faithful to their God. At the height of their greatness as the nation of Israel under King Solomon, they were extremely rich – in fact the richest in the world-, mighty in war, and received tributes from other lands.

Bless him and make his name great.

God blessed Abraham with wealth. He was also named the Hebrew and Abraham of the Most High God after he won against the five kings. God also changed his name from Abram to Abraham, father of many nations. In those lands, Abimelech the king knew him as the blessed one of the Lord and a prophet. To this day, we know him as a friend of God, among other great titles.

Make him a blessing.

Abimelech was blessed for Abram's sake, Lot was blessed and saved from death for Abram's sake, and even in his bloodline, and it was so. Isaac became a blessing to Abimelech and Jacob was a blessing to Laban's household.

While the children of Israel were in Egypt, the nation was expanded and grown for their sake, so that when they left they would be a great nation with much substance as the Lord had promised Abraham.

Those who bless him will be blessed and he who curses him will be cursed.

Abimelech's household suffered barrenness when he took Sarah as his wife. When he returned her and made reparations, Abraham prayed for them and they began to bear again.

To give him seed as the stars of heaven and as the sand of the seashore.

Abraham ended up having 8 sons biologically; all of them were blessed and dispersed except Isaac. We are told that Ishmael had twelve sons, princes of their cities, whom the Lord promised to multiply exceedingly.

Isaac, who was the child of the promise, had two sons who multiplied exceedingly. Israel, God's chosen nation, left as a great multitude from Egypt after entering there numbering only seventy.

In the few instances where the Israelites were numbered, they were a great multitude; even more than the populations of some nations presently.

A multitude as the stars of heaven was a reference to his spiritual lineage, and since Christianity first became until now there have been billions who plead Christ as their King, and are all in the lineage of Abraham, the father of faith. He is the father of faith because he was the first one whose faith was counted to him for righteousness; justification by grace through faith. And not only did he believe for himself, he also had faith to leave that inheritance to all his generations forever.

Promised to give Abraham and his seed the land that they were on forever.

The Lord promised him and his seed the land from the river of Egypt to the river Euphrates. After He delivered them from slavery in Egypt, He led them to it and then led them to conquer it. They occupied most of that land until they rebelled and were carried off into captivity. To this day, they are still fighting to occupy it.

That he would give Abram an heir of his blood.

Sarah was barren so when God told Abram He would bless him, Abraham assumed that his chief servant would be his heir. God said that it would be someone from Abrams' loins. By Sarah's design, Abraham had Ishmael of Hagar; later on, he had Isaac of Sarah.

The Lord chose Isaac as the heir of the promise.

He would be his shield (Protector) and his exceeding great reward (Prosperity).

Abraham never knew any harm from the hand of a human being all his days. In the days when a threat was imminent, the Lord intervened.

He was also prosperous all his days. He had the Blessing on his life that maketh rich and addeth no sorrow with it.

Abraham's seed would be strangers and slaves in a foreign land for 400 years but He would lead them back to their inheritance after that.

They continued to live as strangers in Canaan and in the days of Israel they relocated to Egypt because of famine according to the word of the Lord.

They were slaves in Egypt and when they cried to the Lord, by the hand of Moses He led them out of Egypt and by the hand of Joshua into the Promised Land.

Abraham would live a long life and die in peace.

Abraham lived a long, fruitful life to his old age and died in peace. He died in peace because he had set his affairs in order before he died. His two older sons buried him in the cave at Machpelah.

He would be a God unto him and to his seed forever.

He walked closely with Israel and when they drew far away from Him, He always left a remnant and room for repentance. He also gave them the promise of the Messiah and the establishment of a New Jerusalem.

In Abraham shall all nations of the world be blessed.

In his seed, Jesus Christ the son of David was all the nations of the world blessed and continue to be blessed even now.

The climax of that blessing will be in His second coming when evil and death shall be no more.

Abraham's seed shall possess the gates of his enemies.

The Bible is among other things a record of Israel's conquests against his enemies. Israel conquered all their enemies as long as they lived in obedience and faithfulness to God. Their greatest warring king, David never lost a battle.

"And the gates of hell shall not prevail against you." Even now, Christians are guaranteed that since

fighting must be done victory will always be theirs as long as they stand in the strength and might of the Lord.

* ❖ Do you believe that Jesus Christ is the son of God and the only way to God? Have you confessed to Him?

....
....

* ❖ Do you have any unforgiveness in your heart? TIP- forgiveness is a decision, not a feeling.

....
....
....

* ❖ How are you navigating life and its challenges in the 21st Century?

....
....
....
....
....
....

Part 3: We Are Abraham's Seed and Heirs of The Promise.

How We Came To Be...

The story, like all good stories, begins with a man and a woman who love each other and one would do anything for the other. The scene is set in the most beautiful garden, exquisite in form and functionality. They were placed in it by the Creator to tend, rule over, and grow it into something even more impressive. The greatest task, however, was to maintain the relationship between them and their Maker.

On one fine afternoon, an intruder came into the garden and tricked the woman into committing a grievous sin against their Lord. She, who came out of the man, also convinced the man to sully himself. (James 1:14-16) When the Creator came by to check on His creation he was disappointed. He left the man and woman clothed in His glory, when he came back they were clothed in fig leaves; when he saw them last they were lords over His creation, then their authority and dominion had been usurped by a new prince of this world. They originally were in His image and likeness, but what He saw before Him bore no resemblance to His image or likeness.

He had no choice but to fire them - although it broke His heart- they had broken the rules of occupancy. He made them aware of the new conditions they would be dealing with, seeing as they had chosen to submit to a different lord. He furnished them as well as He could for the journey ahead because He is a loving Master, and then He drove them out of His perfectly made garden to fend for themselves in the untamed earth.

Because He loved them so and was certain that given an opportunity to be reconnected to Him, they would choose it, He left them with a promise of the Seed of a woman, who would be able to beat down the head of the serpent, the subtle deceiver.

Humankind is a composite of three distinct parts; Spirit, Soul, and Body. Thanks to the error of Adam and Eve, the spirit of man was disconnected from the Spirit of God and therefore suffered an instant catastrophic death (separation from God is death. Man no longer bore the image and likeness of God, because he was no longer born of the Spirit. (Genesis 6:3) The link was severed, but the seed remained.

The soul that was initially submitted to the spirit that was submitted to the Spirit of God lost its Lordship and was subject to a new corrupt spirit, which is the prince of this world. It was therefore subject to corruption and iniquity. It lost its dominion and authority; what man was convinced into thinking was promotion into godlikeness was a demotion into slave hood. The introduction of things like fear, lust, selfishness, and anger was made possible.

The body was no longer subject to a soul that was under the counsel of the Spirit of God. Since it is the Spirit that gives life, decay, and expiration became the fate of the physical body. What was initially for man the body of their glorification became the body of their humiliation. (Philippians 3:21)

As highlighted above, Elohim was not pleased with the fall of man; He had a particular purpose for the creation of this creature that was of the earth earthy, yet filled with the glory of heaven. So He left an opportunity for redemption and over the years succeeding that, the plan came more and more into focus.

Questions.

❖ Why do you think God asked Adam and Eve, *"Who told you you were naked"*?

....
....
....
....
....
....
....

❖ In the beginning, what did God mean when He said *"Let us make man in our image, after our likeness"*?

....
....
....
....
....
....
....
....

....
....
....
....
....

❖ What was the original sin?

....
....
....
....
....
....
....
....
....
....
....
....
....
....

Christ Our Qualifier.

Try all you want, you could never separate Christ from anything. Any thought you might have; of greatness, knowledge, wisdom, salvation, eternal life, riches, honour, life, achievement; they are all subject to the wisdom and power of God who is Christ Jesus (1st Cor.1:24-30). It is in Him and by Him and through Him that all things were made (Colossians 1:16,17); if you can think about it, the Alpha, the Beginning of it, is Christ. Therefore, it is only right that we explore how we come into our inheritance from the role of Christ; the promised Seed.

The spirit of man was separated from the Spirit of God and therefore died. So there was a cavernous space left in man where the Spirit of God filled, that emptiness just ached and the enemy because he had managed to convince them to rebel, the spirit of rebellion could move in, the spirit of sin. It is why the Bible says that all descendants of Adam are born in sin, because all are born with the spirit of sin in them as the inheritance they obtain from their parents. From the beginning, God had a great plan and purpose for man (Ephesians 2:10) that was delayed by the serpent in the Garden of Eden, but not deterred. The seed left in man is evident in the way that by the second generation, we see Abel and Cain going before the Lord to offer a sacrifice; there is a space in man that only God can fit into. We also in this story see the corruption of the enemy in how Cain is warned of sin crouching at the door of his heart and he goes ahead to let it in to rule him.

There was a plan for redemption; we see it in the moment when it is recorded that men began calling upon the Lord, and he always came to their aid. By the time we get to Abraham and he walks with the Lord, we see worship and honour when he offered a tithe to Melchizedek, king of Salem, whom we are told had neither ancestors nor genealogy (Hebrews 7:3). It is the Almighty power of God demonstrated because one man and his household managed to dismay five kings with their armies.

The sacrifice on Mount Moriah is a foreshadowing of the sacrificial love of Christ demonstrated in Him choosing to die on the cross, to redeem us (Hebrews 9:12), not by the blood of animals but by His priceless blood that washes all and makes white as snow. So if we believe in our hearts and confess with our tongues that Jesus Christ is Lord, we are saved.

Let us begin exploring from the point that we are saved, and justified, and the Spirit of God indwells us. All this can happen only through the sacrifice of Christ on the cross and our faith in the finished works that He wrought when He descended into the dead, was glorified ascended into Heaven, and is now seated at the right hand of the Father. He is resting, His work was perfected; He is clothed as both judge and priest, both king and friend, and His outlook are both ancient and eternal (Revelation 1:13). The new man born of the Spirit CANNOT sin and is counted righteous before

God (1st John 3:9), therefore the relationship was restored, and man could once again bear the image and likeness of God.

Questions.

- ❖ What does it mean that one born of the Spirit cannot sin?

  ....
  ....
  ....
  ....
  ....
  ...

- ❖ Why do you think it was significant that Isaac made it to the altar of sacrifice before the Lord opened Abraham's eyes to see the ram?

  ....
  ....
  ....
  ....
  ....

- ❖ Why do you think Jesus' sacrifice was the only one that sufficed?

  ....
  ....
  ....
  ....
  ....
  ....

Jesus Christ the Son of Abraham.

When we look at Christ as the Son of Man, His genealogy was traced back to Him being the son of David and also the son of Abraham (Matthew 1:1-17). We are also told that while Abraham gave a tithe to Melchizedek the priest of the most High God, his entire generation was in his loins (Hebrews 7:1-10). So Christ as the son of Abraham tithed to the priest of the Most High and is also now seated in Heaven forever as the High Priest after the order of Melchizedek. Christ as the son of God received the tithe from the hand of Moses, and is in heaven now as King, receiving all our sacrifices- worship, thanksgiving, praise, gifts- and tithes.

God promised Abraham *(Genesis 12:3):*
> *"I will bless those who bless you*
> *And curse the one who curses you;*
> *And all the families of the earth*
> *Shall bless themselves by you."*

The seed that was promised to the woman in the beginning then became the one promised to Abraham because all families of the earth were to bless themselves through him and his progeny. (Galatians 3:16)

❖ Why was it important for Christ's genealogy to be highlighted in the scripture?

....

....

....

....

....

<u>We are Abraham's Seed.</u>

*"Even as Abraham believed God, and it was accounted to him for righteousness. **Know ye therefore that they which are of faith, the same are the children of Abraham**. And the scripture, foreseeing that God would justify the heathen through faith, preached before the gospel unto Abraham, saying, **In thee shall all nations be blessed**. So then they which be of faith are blessed with faithful Abraham." -Galatians 3:6-9(KJV)*

We have already established that those who are born of the Spirit are re-connected to God, that Christ was rejected by God so that once again we could be accepted back into God's fold, and that by having faith in Him, we have a way to relate with God. We have also established that God's primary role for man was the management of His earthly creation. In Genesis 2:5, the scriptures explain that the reason why nothing was growing and the Lord hadn't sent the rain yet was that there was nobody to work the land. The Garden of Eden was created for man, not man for the garden, so all that was added therein had to be exactly right for man to thrive in. Hence He created man and instructed them to have dominion; to use the Garden of Eden as a learning place and a pilot program, and then replicate it throughout the earth. Here was the first recorded covenant in history; between God and Adam, when He gave him control of the garden, and in turn Adam and his descendants were to keep the counsel of God.

Those who are born of God and adopted into son ship through Jesus Christ (Ephesians 1:4-6), then require a new way to reclaim their dominion, rightful ownership, and inheritance of the earth. It is only by having access to this that you can build careers, families, businesses, have good health, have a healthy relationship with the Father, and then leave all these as an inheritance for your future generations.

Remember we highlighted earlier that Adam surrendered his rightful dominion of the earth to the prince of this world? - mean the devil- Apart from God coming up with our solution to death, decay, and corruption, where our souls would be saved from eternal damnation, He also came up with a way to restore our dominion here on earth. The plan was seeded in Abraham, when He believed and it was counted to him for righteousness.

The Lord Himself said in His word: *"The heaven, even the heavens, are the LORD's: But the earth hath he given to the children of men." - Psalm 115:16.*

When we receive Christ, we also become the seed of Abraham by faith, because Abraham was justified by grace because he believed, as we are. Therefore all the blessings that were on Abraham are also due to us, we are liable to claim them for ourselves.

"And if ye be Christ's, then are ye Abraham's seed, and heirs according to the promise."-Galatians 3:29

Let us now look at a few of the promises and the promise of their fulfilment in our lives in scripture.

Make Abraham a great nation.

All who believe in Christ the Messiah, in all corners of the earth, in all ages and eons, are the seed of Abraham by faith. Therefore he truly is the father of nations, and as sure as you cannot count the stars in the sky, neither can you number his descendants (Romans 9:7-8). They are of all races and nationalities, all skin tones and build; they live in diverse climates with the uniting factor being Christ. What's more, Christ promised in Matthew 8:11 that many would come from all corners of the earth and sit with Abraham, Isaac, and Jacob in the Kingdom of Heaven. Each of us also has an opportunity to grow into great nations, by having spheres of influence and raising generations for the Lord.

Bless him and make his name great.

We have the promise that our names are to be great. A person's name is great when they have wealth, status, or achievement of a sort, what people associate your name with. Your name can be great in your community, country, continent, or even the entire world. In Deut. 28:13 we are the head and not the tail, above only and never beneath, Proverbs 22:1 tells us that a good name is better than riches. In the New Testament, we see Jesus promising His disciples that when the Holy Spirit came upon them they would do great things. Great deeds followed great men like Paul the apostle (Acts

19:11-12), and the greater promise was that Christ promised we would do greater things than He did, by faith. (John 14:12)

Make him a blessing.

A blessing blesses those around them, and for us Christians, the first way of blessing others is witnessing to them and leading them to The Truth (Acts 3:25-27). The scriptures also teach us that to be a blessing is to bless even those who curse us and to continue to inherit the blessing (1 Peter 3:9).

He would be a God unto him and to his seed forever.

Our God is a god of the living (Matt 22:32), we are exalted with Christ in heaven, and after the mortal body expires, we shall be re-joined to Him in eternity. Even now He is our God, the only one who deserves our worship, honour, and adoration. He is our God indeed, He watches over us, provides for our every need in Christ Jesus, and gives us victory and prosperity.

Abraham's seed shall possess the gates of his enemies.

Christ possessed the gates of the enemy when he triumphed over all principalities and powers (Colossians 2:15). As He was the forerunner for us, by faith we also possess that victory against our great enemy, and in practice we only work to possess the victory already won for us by Christ. (2 Corinthians 2:14)

"And I say also unto thee, That thou art Peter, and upon this rock I will build my church; and the gates of hell shall not prevail against it."- Matthew 16:18

Questions.

❖ Go back to Part 2 of the book, look at the promises that we have not covered above, and prove with scripture how they are due to us.

....

....

....

....

....

....

❖ Which of the promises above would be most useful to you in life currently?

....

....

....

....

....

....

....

....

....

How We Obtain The Promise.

After the general understanding that the blessing of Abraham is due to us because we are his seed by faith, the next step is for each person to personalise them. That is the way to translate them into a working force in your life because the Word of God is His tool of creation and what He sends to fulfil His purpose here on earth. Therefore accepting that Word in your life, with the wisdom and power accompanying it ensures possession.

The principles are:

Appropriation- It is taking on something that was originally meant for someone else and claiming it as yours. This is what we should do with the blessings of Abraham, after we believe and confess that Christ became a curse with our curse we may enjoy the blessing of Abraham who was blessed in all things. The statement then changes from *"God promised Abraham to make his name great"*, to *"The Lord has promised to make my name great"*.

Submission- Those who are led by the Spirit of God, are the sons of God. To be part of the Kingdom of citizenry therefore demands submission to the Lordship of the Holy Spirit in our lives. We must also submit to the physical authorities that the Lord has placed in our lives; fathers to bless us, mothers to teach and instruct us, pastors and teachers to lead us to all truth. We must also submit to the authority of the scripture, if you read and do not do, the Bible says that it is a waste of time (James 4:17) The only way to obtain the promise of God is by knowing what it is, and the only way of knowing what it is by learning from His word; read your Bible like it is the key to everything you desire because it is.

Maturity- Paul quarrelled with the Hebrew Christians in Hebrews 5:12-14, that while they had the advantage of learning God's word in the Torah before salvation, they were not growing. Here he highlighted an important principle; maturity is attained through practice. The practiced word is so that the mind can be transformed through renewing, to the point where the old rebellious nature in you is subdued and the soul can then fully submit to the leading of the spirit, and instruct the flesh accordingly.

Galatians 4:1-3 also teaches us that while an heir is still a child, they cannot be in charge of the inheritance. Children are more in tune with the flesh and seek to satisfy their lusts, so they fall into the realm of "and *God can satisfy your every need according to His riches in glory in Christ Jesus*". They aren't trusted with any responsibility without supervision because the works of the flesh are still manifest in them, and in the battle between spirit and flesh more often than not it is the spirit that is beaten down instead of the flesh being beaten into submission. Such a person is double-minded; there is always a tug-of-war between what the Lord says and what their flesh wants to do at the moment, and the Bible says such a person is unstable in all his ways.

So the reason we have teachers, pastors, apostles, prophets, and evangelists is so that they can hurry us up in the process of maturity to the point where God can trust us with responsibility. And where God sends you, He sends you with resources and grace to fulfil.

Humility- We should model the example of Christ who humbled Himself and left His station in heaven to come and live on earth as a mere man just so He can fulfil the purpose of the Father (Philippians 2:6-11); He humbled Himself and was obedient even unto death. The result of it was that God highly exalted Him. The way up is down, God gives grace to a humble heart and pushes away the proud. Humility is to be more and more like Christ, to take on the form of a servant to obtain the promise. We are told in scripture that while Canaan was promised to Abraham, he never owned an inch of it. Rich as he was, with options for other lands, he stayed there as a squatter on the land because the Lord told him to.

Questions.

❖ How are you an heir of the promise?

....

....

....

....

....

....

....

....

....

....

....

....

....

....

....

❖ If the church has all the answers, then why are there still so many questions in the world?

....

....

....

....

....

....

....

....

❖ Are you pursuing purpose, or struggling to survive?

....

....

....

....

The Manifestation of the Promise in Our Lives.

There are sixty-three mentions of Abraham in the New Testament, all connected to faith and promise. It qualifies over and over again that Abraham was justified by grace through faith; he was counted righteous because he believed in the God who called him out of his father's house. He walked with this great God and goodness and mercy followed him all the days of his life. He obtained the promise because he believed that the God who promised was also able to do. (Romans 4:1-16) The ways God trained Abraham in faith and faithfulness was to ask for sacrifices from Him.

There are five main sacrifices Abraham offered to the Lord: Firstly, he left his country of origin, with everything and everyone he had gotten used to and he credited for his success and wellbeing to follow the God of glory who spoke to him. Secondly, he left his father's house and all his; his safety net and security, the people he could count on to march to battle with and for him, and who would bury him when he was finally gathered up. Thirdly, he had to give up Ishmael. After so many years of hoping and believing for a child of his own bowels, when he finally had him, God was like *you gotta let him go*. Finally, and the one we all know, is his willingness to offer Isaac as burnt offering on the altar of the Lord. Each sacrifice demanded more faith from him, a greater degree of surrender to the

Lord, and that he let go of all the earthly securities he though he needed. It is almost like God needed him to understand how little everything else means in order to trust him with loyal covenantal love and security that only the Lord could offer. Abraham on the other hand needed to be broken within him; he needed to get to the point where all of him was remoulded by God before he could be trusted with the fate of all humanity.

Faith demands sacrifice; in the present continuous sense. If you want more, you should be willing to lose more; on the flip side you gain more in the process. And respect time; God's timing as well as the time it takes for you to learn the way you should walk. Abram met the God of glory who along the way made Himself known to him as Jireh, ElRoi, Almighty, Lord, as time progressed and they related more. Be patient with yourself dear.

One of the most honouring statements that the Lord made about Abraham is in Genesis 18:19, *"For I know him, that he will command his children and his household after him, and they shall keep the way of the LORD, to do justice and judgment; that the LORD may bring upon Abraham that which he hath spoken of him."* This implies that the promise of God may be upon your life, but there are protocols associated with its manifestation and establishment in your life. The primary one is faithfulness to God; as He is faithful to fulfil His part of the covenant, so should you be. A Testament is a contract; the Bible is, among other things, a contractual agreement between God and His people.

Faithfulness is joined to a few pieces that we will discuss below:

Proclamation is extremely important because it is essentially laying hold of the hope set before us (Hebrews 6:15-18). It owns the word of God, making it personal. One of my favourite scriptures to proclaim is 2 Corinthians 9:8 and this is how I usually say it " *And God is ABLE to make ALL GRACE abound toward me, so that at ALL times and in ALL ways, HAVING ALL sufficiency, I may abound to ALL good works.*"
The more you proclaim, the more you have scripture to meditate upon, and the more you can make your way prosperous, and have good success.

Do not be stubborn, needing to be led around by a bridle, do not seek to walk your way after you have found The Way. You see, our trust in God is demonstrated in how much we are willing to follow as He leads, how much of what we hold dear we are willing to give up or surrender to Him, and how hard we work to do what He has instructed us to do, without knowing what the result will be. Faithfulness, in essence, is our response to how much we trust God; His word says that His plans for us are always good, but do you believe that enough to follow Him even through the valley of the shadow of death?

"I will instruct you and teach you in the way you should go; I will counsel you with my loving eye on you.

Do not be like the horse or the mule, which have no understanding but must be controlled by bit and bridle or they will not come to you."- Psalm 32:8-9

Study to show yourself approved. We have learned above that maturity is attained by learning and practicing. Likewise, mastery is attained by study and practice. (James 2:24, 2nd Timothy 2:15) Learn the Word of God, pick out the revelation and wisdom in it, and apply it to your life. If you are having a challenge in any area of your life, go to the Word of God to discover the Truth about it. The truth is the word of God concerning it; learn that and then meditate upon it to discover the revelation in it. Use that revelation to then stir the gift of God within you, to the point where a refined plan of action bubbles up from within you, and then walk the Way laid out before you. Always remember that the Lord has hidden treasures in His word, and it is the profit of a prince to search them out; never stop!

Pursue purpose, not necessity- Seek to fulfil the Lord's will here on earth because God follows His word to make sure it comes to pass and nothing else. Fit yourself as a tool for the working of the Lord's word and He will provide all the means necessary for the word to come to pass. And while you are doing that, beware of deception that could lead you back into focusing on yourself rather than Christ.

Take advantage of opportunities you are presented with. After you have prayed, believing the Bible says that you have received (Mark 11:24). Walk this earth knowing that God has already answered every prayer you have ever said believing. When we pray for success, He presents us with an opportunity to make our names great, when we pray for wealth, He gives us the ability to make wealth, when we pray for prosperity, He releases upon us the blessing that makes rich, and adds no sorrow with it. God always gives us seed, because HE built within us the system of productivity that receives a seed and grows it into something that bears fruit. It is in the great commission of Genesis 1:28; that He said you ARE fruitful! Become the productive nature that births ideas, multiplies what it produces, then with what it has multiplied it fills the earth and rules it. So whether or not you do something with your life, you ARE fruitful; so why not do great exploits with the gift of God upon your life?

Conclusion.

We have walked the journey of the life of Abraham together, and have seen how he came to be the father of faith and a friend of God. We have learned the demands of faith, and the steps to maturity. Highlighted is also the place of obedience in a person's relationship with God. We obey because we do not yet have the complete picture and we trust the author of the map of life to guide our steps to our preordained destinations.

I think the greatest takeaway for me however is that God has loyal love for His children, and He expresses it through showing us kindness and consideration, defending us from our enemies, giving us wisdom, making us rich, and the greatest show of it is being with us always. His promises are forever; He has no plan of changing that therefore we can hold on to that constant in a world and a life that is constantly going through changes.

It is my sincere prayer that these words have transformed your mind, as the word of the Lord always does. I pray the Lord bless you and keep you, answer you when you call, expand your territory, and instruct you in the way to expanding the expanses of your reach.

Shalom!

The Preacher is a Prophet, not a Puppet,
The Preacher must get the vision that:
        The Pulpit is a Throne, not a Prison.

Bibliography

Unger, F, Merrill. <u>The New Unger's Bible Dictionary</u>.
Chicago: Moody Press, 1957.